The Ghosts of Birds

poems by

Kristina Marie Darling

Finishing Line Press
Georgetown, Kentucky

The Ghosts of Birds

Copyright © 2017 by Kristina Marie Darling
ISBN 978-1-63534-157-7 First Edition
All rights reserved under International and Pan-American Copyright Conventions.
No part of this book may be reproduced in any manner whatsoever without written permission from the publisher, except in the case of brief quotations embodied in critical articles and reviews.

Publisher: Leah Maines

Editor: Christen Kincaid

Artwork: Kristin Giordano

Photo of Kristina Darling: Linda Darling

Photo of Kristin Giordano: Kristin Giordano

Cover Design: Elizabeth Maines McCleavy

Printed in the USA on acid-free paper.
Order online: www.finishinglinepress.com
        also available on amazon.com

                Author inquiries and mail orders:
                      Finishing Line Press
                        P. O. Box 1626
               Georgetown, Kentucky 40324
                          U. S. A.

"The absence of eternity is not simply a limit that is thought, but a lack that is felt at the heart of temporal experience. The limiting idea then becomes the sorrow proper to the negative."

—Paul Ricoeur, TIME AND NARRATIVE

$$f_1(A) - f_1(AA) + \frac{1}{2}f_1(Aa) = p^2 + pq(p+q) = p = f_0(A)$$

It was a year of many discoveries. First a cold shore, then the smallness of the bones. Of course there were people who set sail on the desolation ships. For them, it was merely an opportunity, not a disturbance of any kind.

And the burial that failed to satisfy anyone. Not even a hand to place on the casket, or a body to rest beside the thistle plants

Come   flocks strangest follow
me morning towers form &
melt sky sea dark clouds
grey green grow wash shore
   clump black lace   rocks
                    wet
lone west ship chunks beach
         cliff things waves
pine knee-
    man deep   blue trunks

After an entire winter of non-address, you still didn't want me posting letters. When I seal the envelope, everything comes apart in my hands.

Together, we try to reassemble the ghost. Her body is intricate and all of the books are far away. Now a ship that passes us by again and again.

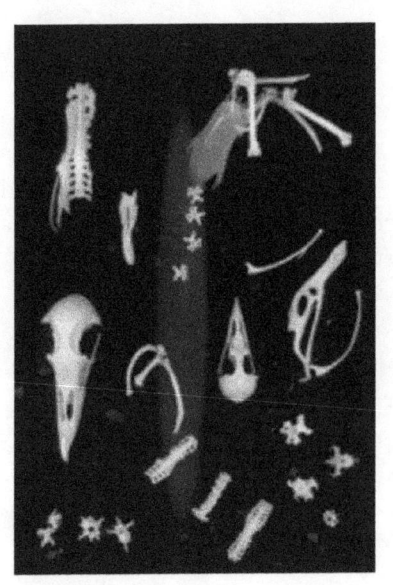

And there is no barge in the white envelope that appears beneath my door. The thin shores already sealed with frost. When will the postman arrive and what little failures will he carry.

Shhhhhh. The doorbell is ringing. To whom should I address this?

                    To you who held out your hand—

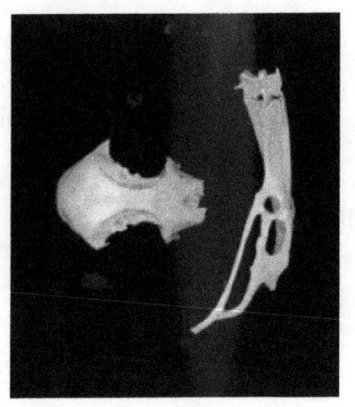

More and more, I'm convinced those were the last ships coming.

Around me the harbor is dark. Your letters are still held up in customs. An unarticulated melancholy, a sea.

                                          When the tide falls away we will each board a different ferry to shore.

The little bones that arrive with your letters. These I do not label or inspect. They just appear they come undone they stutter.

The sea, as always, unannounced. No frost or distant voice to warn us.

There will be no dispatch from the other coast.

The tiny ships I carried for you, the ships that I built for you out of only the bones.

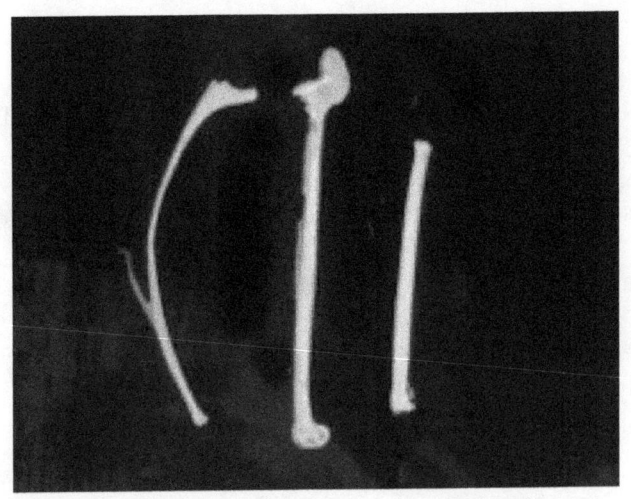

My letters, tied with white string in the hull of a ship that never reached the other coast.

My letters, which startled the very bird I was trying to describe as I stood before the impasse.

Now that bird will never come back. We may die writing each other from adjoining rooms.

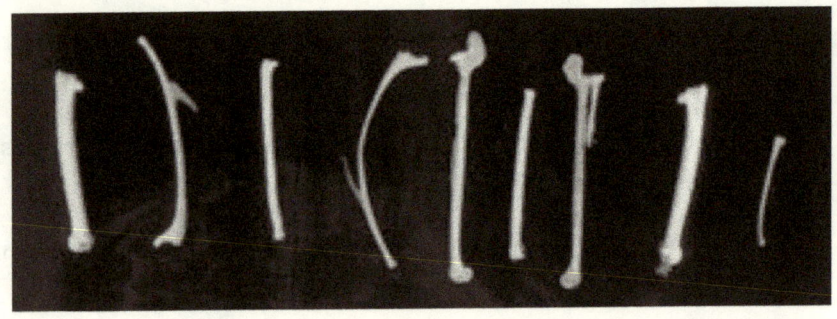

The ocean grew larger and larger.

The distance between rooms smaller.

We hear their voices in the corridor, an aperture a mouth to cover and close.

This heap of ash, this terror.

No barge empty enough to carry it all.

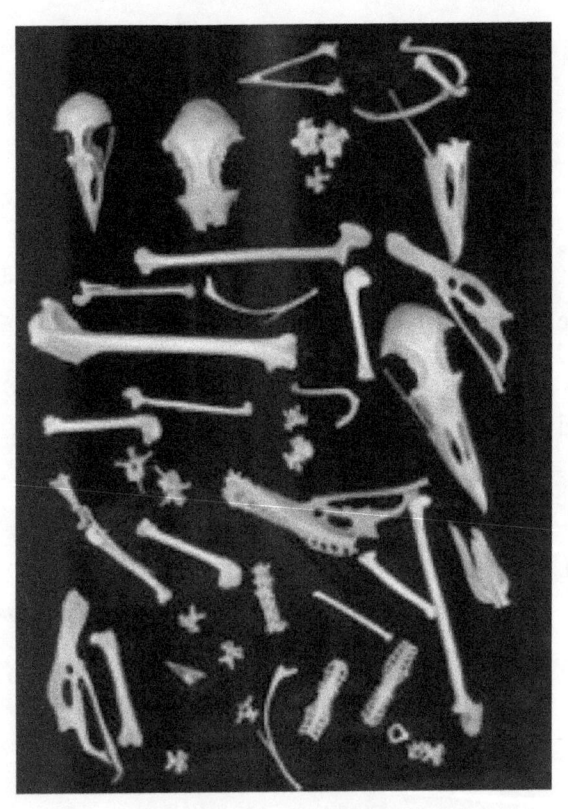

The last snowfall the last thaw.   Your letters widowed into dust.

Now, a little burial.

Your grief even smaller.

Did you place the bones near each other.   Here or here.

When I'm not waiting for the ships I listen for you.

When I'm not waiting.

In such a light how could you say

No, there is no ship that waits like that.

Kristina Marie Darling is the author of over twenty collections of poetry, which include X MARKS THE DRESS (2013, with Carol Guess), FORTRESS (2014), GHOST / LANDSCAPE (2016, with John Gallaher), and DARK HORSE (2017), forthcoming from C & R Press. Her books have been described by literary critics as "haunting," "mesmerizing," and "complex." Poet and Kenyon Review editor Zach Savich writes that her body of work is a "singularly graceful and stunningly incisive exploration of poetic insight, vision, and transformation." Donald Revell writes of her SELECTED POEMS, "Here is a new tradition, alive in bright air." Kristina's books have also been reviewed widely in literary magazines, including The Boston Review, Ploughshares, The Iowa Review, The Colorado Review, The Mid-American Review, Pleiades, and The Southern Humanities Review.

Within the past few years, her writing has been honored with two Yaddo residencies, a Hawthornden Castle Fellowship, multiple residencies at the American Academy in Rome, and a Visiting Researcher Fellowship from the University of Washington's Helen R. Whiteley Center. She has also held artist-in-residence fellowships at the Ucross Foundation, the Helene Wurlitzer Foundation, the Kimmel Harding Nelson Center for the Arts, the Caldera Foundation, the Atlantic Center for the Arts, the Writer's Room at the Betsy Hotel – South Beach, the I-Park Foundation, the Hambidge Center for the Creative Arts and Sciences, the Virginia Center for the Creative Arts, the Brush Creek Foundation for the Arts, the Vermont Studio Center, the Ragdale Foundation, and numerous other institutions. Kristina is the recipient of international literary arts fellowships from the B.A.U. Institute and 360 Xochi Quetzal, as well as grants from

Harvard University's Kittredge Fund, the Whiting Foundation, the Elizabeth George Foundation, the Ora Lerman Trust, the Regional Arts Commission of St. Louis, and the Rockefeller Archive Center. She was also awarded a Morris Fellowship in the Arts. Her work has been recognized three times with the Dan Liberthson Prize from the Academy of American Poets. She has received nominations for the National Book Award, the National Book Critics Circle Award, the PEN/Diamonstein-Spielvogel Award, and the Kingsley Tufts Award.

Kristina is active as a literary critic, with reviews and essays appearing in such magazines as The Gettysburg Review, The Los Angeles Review of Books, Agni, The Boston Review, The Colorado Review, Pleiades: A Journal of New Writing, and New Letters. Her first book of criticism is under contract with C & R Press. An excerpt of this forthcoming work was honored with a nomination for the Nona Balakian Citation for Excellence in Reviewing. Her critical projects have been supported by grants from the University of Missouri and the University at Buffalo, as well as a Riverrun Foundation Research Fellowship to complete archival work at Yale University's Beinecke Rare Book and Manuscript Library. Kristina holds degrees in English Literature and American Culture Studies from Washington University, as well as an M.A. in Philosophy from the University of Missouri. She is currently working toward both an M.F.A. in Poetry at New York University and a Ph.D. in English Literature at S.U.N.Y.-Buffalo. She is Editor-in-Chief of Tupelo Quarterly, Founding Editor-in-Chief of Noctuary Press, and Grants Specialist at Black Ocean.

Kristin Giordano is a photographer based in Tacoma, WA. She works mainly with antique and experimental cameras. Exhibitions include New York University, Abu Dhabi; the Kittredge Gallery, Tacoma, WA; the Collins Memorial Library at the University of Puget Sound, Tacoma, WA; Fulcrum Gallery, Tacoma, WA; and the Museum of Contemporary Art (MOCA) in Tucson, AZ. Her work is in numerous public and private collections, including the collection of the Photographic Center Northwest. Awards include a 2008 project grant from Qatar University, a 2011 Print Sponsorship award from the Photographic Center Northwest, and a 2011 and 2015 TAIP Artist Project Grant. Her recent series "Landscape and Transformation: Photographs of Doha, Qatar 2008-2010" was selected as a finalist in PhotoLucida's Critical Mass portfolio contest, and a selection of her photographs was featured in the journal Guernica. Recent public art projects in Tacoma, WA include the installation Charismatic Megafauna and the Spaceworks mural Humans, Join US!™

www.ingramcontent.com/pod-product-compliance
Lightning Source LLC
LaVergne TN
LVHW040118080426
835507LV00041B/1808